MAP OF THE ATLANTIC SLAVE TRADE ROUTE

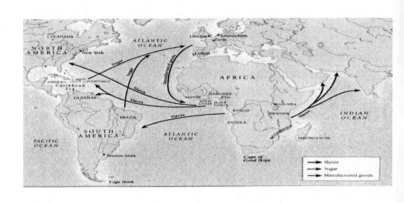

TWISTED

A book of historical chronicles relating to the African Holocaust of the 15th Century, more commonly known as: "The Atlantic Slave Trade!"

More than just a book of poems…

BY KEMET IMANI

Acknowledgements

"LEST WE FORGET!"

This book is first and foremost dedicated to
OUR ANCESTORS, on whose shoulders we stand.
For if it were not for them, we most surely would not have
been here today!

Acknowledgements to:

THE MOST HIGH ONE, Grand Creator and Master of the
Universe- of all things tangible and intangible.

To my Mother- Noreen Browne and my Father-
Collin Carter. Thank you both for bestowing upon me the
Wisdom, Knowledge, and Inner-Standing of always
remembering our glorious kingdoms and painful past.

To my Foster Mother Claire Ewen, for always letting me
know: "I can do anything great." Thank you for believing in
me. Love you loads.

To my children: Chellon, Chenade, Prince-Chemari, and
Prince-Chekhai.

To my Grand-Children: Princess-Nyah-Chanti (thank you so
much for your contribution, writing poem No: 30) Princess-

Narea, Princess-Sanai, Prince-Shai and
The Newborn Princess- Nylah-Reign.

To my King Keith (Stamina) Lawrence: Thank you for being
there when I need you. You are my rock. To
My Stepdaughter, Shereen Lawrence, who constantly reminds
me: "Seven brothers, seven different minds!" ☺·☒

To Mama-Adjua, my greatest inspiration in relation to this
book. Thank you for pushing my mind, heart, and spirit just
to get this book done for a much needed cause. "If it were not
for you, this book may never have got written."

To my two publicists Sistar Gail Henry and Brother
Menelik (John) Sandiford. Illustrator Jason Browne. Empress
Claudette (R.I.E.P) who insisted that I write a poem about
the Drum and to make the Libation poem a little longer- so
I did☺, and to HRH Alf (My Vincey Brother) thank you for
your continuous support.

To all my Nieces and Nephews, Grand Nephews, Grand
Nieces, God-children and Friends alike-
Carol Soverall especially.

A special shout to Dr. Ava Eagle Brown #themangogirl
who took this and finished the last lap for me to get this book
published. Thank you for tolerating me as I know that I can
be a handful!

To all of you who I have not mentioned personally but who
have supported me in getting this book to its final tangible

state. I could have never done it without you all. You are whom I call my: "Chosen Few" no matter what the cause, you few are always sure to support me unconditionally. You know who you are, and your kindness will always be remembered from the bottom of my heart. I love you all loads! Xx

PREFACE

During this time of 2020, having just celebrated October 2019 in Mama Africa for "The Year of Return," I was led to continuously remember the journey of the enslaved and how we became the children of the diaspora.

We can no longer believe that we are born into this world, simply to accommodate wealth and status, without recognising those who came before us and what they had to endure for our survival, henceforth allowing for our mere presence here today.

It was an honour and privilege to write this book of poetry on behalf of our Ancestors. Hence, wanting all who will read it to know that I am simply a vessel, to channel what comes to me from the Ancestors to you. It was written by our Ancestors, for you, through me (Kemet Imani)

This work is a historical account of some of the inhumane acts/treatments of which captured Africans had to endure; from the heart of Africa to the so-called: "New world!"

The series of events written in this book are based on some of the most disturbing, horrific, and traumatising injustices ever placed on a particular race and its nations; that of the

African holocaust vis à vi the Atlantic Slave Trade. We know that even more horrific episodes happened during this era. Many of the most heinous crimes against humanity- acts way to horrific and soul disturbing to mention in the contents of this book. However, it is my duty to tell what was revealed to me in its truest form.

The Ancestors has shown me (Kemet Imani) that- "In the progression of one's self, one must grow in the comprehension of truth and integrity!" and it is on this premise that I stand.

Told in a poetic form as revealed to me by the Ancestors, them telling: "Their Story!"

> *"Until the Lion tells his side of the story,*
> *tales of the hunt will glorify the hunter!"*

African Proverb

The experiences in this book are "The truth, the whole truth and nothing but the truth: "Lest we Forget!"

From our Ancestors to You!

TABLE OF CONTENTS

TWISTED

Thoughts portrayed from the ideals of others

Wondering minds just to discover

Inconsequential, insignificant, ways of life

Solely created by way of design

Traditions of old lost, and new ones created

Effortlessly loathed, so extreme is the hatred

Deliberately twisted, now into something so sacred

1: THE RUNAWAY

It's been three whole days
Since escaping Jones' plantation
Mama telling me not to leave
But I did without hesitation

You see…
None of us were born
To be shackled day and night
Working like an OX
Whipped and hung
This can't be right?

I had to take my chances
And escape the white man's kingdom
Alone in the woods
I would find my way to freedom

My thoughts led my feet
And I finally fled
Willing and knowingly
That I could end up dead

There I was
6 weeks in…
Deceiving trails of hounds
And horseback men

I would sleep in the days
And travel by night
Easier that way
To keep my hue out of sight

Following the North Star
As I had often seen in Africa
Doubt it would take me there
But I'll settle for Canada

How long will it take me?
Only Oshun and others know
I have to stay to the edge
Where the great river flows

It was hard sustaining energy
As most were taken up with fear
Ssshhhhh!... Stay Still!
I hear the hounds drawing near!

I hide wait and pray
Hoping that the hounds will pass
Without sniffing my trail
Which I hoped would not last

Elders had taught me
The deterrents of the woods
I'm trying hard to remember
 …As I know that I should

I forgot…
Then I remember …

If you ever forget
Nature's plan
Call to the ancestors
To lend a hand
So I did…

Ancestors! Oh Ancestors!
Of Love and Light
Help me through
This desperate plight!
I am not sure
Whether near nor far
But help me to reach
That northern star!

I lost count of the days
And the weeks of travelling
All that I knew
It was early one morning

I looked up and saw
A smiling face
A beautiful Queen
Saying:
You made it… you're safe

But how? I questioned
With teary filled eyes
All I remember
Is dark starry skies

She replied:

That's all you should know
My sweet darling dear
But never, ever forget-
Your ancestors
Brought you here…

2: GOOD OLE' UNCLE TOM

MASSA: Tom!

TOM: Yes Massa

MASSA: How the crops going?
TOM: They going good Massa
                Shall I do some more sowing?
                Or get more slaves to growing?

MASSA: You're so good Tom
TOM: Thank you Massa
                Like a real slave outta
                Do you want some water?
MASSA: No…just bring me your daughter

                GOOD OLE UNCLE TOM

MASSA: Tom! Tom!
                I'm feeling very sick
TOM: Oh, my Lordy!!
                Let's hurry and get us fixed

TOM: Mary-Lou we very sick
                Go and get the herbs
MARY-LOU: But Uncle Tom…
                You look fine to me
                So why call me the nurse?

TOM:	It's Massa Lou- we very sick
	So hurry up and come
MARY-LOU:	OK I'll get the herbs for him
	Wait there I'll bring you some
TOM:	Oh Massa Sir Lou on her way
	To make us well and better
MASSA:	Just call her now!
	Tom! You fool!
	Go right away! Go get her!
TOM:	Oh Massa Sir Yes I will
	I'll go and get her now
	I'm gonna be so very quick
	First let me wipe your brow

GOOD OLE UNCLE TOM

TOM:	Mary-Lou! Please come quick
	As we about to die
MARY-LOU:	I'll make the process quicker Tom
	Keep it up! I tell no lie!
	You running behind Massa
	Like he truly cares 'bout you
	Damn Massa and Ole Uncle Tom
	Two crazy grey-haired fools!
TOM:	She here now Massa

Now drink this quick
This sure to make us better

MASSA:

Just leave me alone
Your piece of S**t
I hate you all…
You Niggas!!!!

GOOD OLE UNCLE TOM!!!

3: COME HERE, PET

MAMA: Lilly-Sue! Lilly-Sue!
                       I have a new pet for you

LILLY –SUE: For me Mama?
                       That's really great
                       But please don't let it
                       Be more than eight

MAMA: No! No! It's under nine
                       I ensured and did
                       What you specified
                       A Negro child
                       Nine years and under
                       With nappy hair
                       That's strong as thunder

LILLY SUE: I can tie a leash
                       To its plaits
                       Or around its neck
                       But not too slack
                       I will never let it go astray
                       And walk it
                       Every night and day

LILLY SUE: Where is it Mama?
                       I'm so excited!

MAMA: Right here my love

Go and get united

LILLY SUE: Oh my Mama…
              What an adorable Pickinnynie
              For a nigga child
              It sure is pretty

LILLY SUE: Now…
              What should I name you?
              My special pet
              Nappy, Coal
              Or maybe jet?

LILLY SUE: That's it… I know
              Just what to call you
              From now on
              You'll be called:
              "My Nappy Blue!"

LILLY SUE: Your Nappy hair
              I love it so
              And your dark blue skin
              Like burnt charcoal

LILLY SUE: Who would had thought?
              The perfect pet
              And one that does
              Not need a vet

LILLY SUE: Nappy-Blue

I will feed you my leftovers
And dress you in bows
With torn clothes
And old covers

LILLY SUE: And If I'm upset
Or angry too
I know I can take it
Out on you

LILLY SUE: I know you won't mind
A friend so true
It would be your pleasure
Dear Nappy-Blue

LILLY SUE: You can sleep on the floor
Right next to my bed
Oh my Nappy-Blue pet
Forever my friend!

4: CRICK CRACK THAT RAGGEDY SHIP

Crick Crack, that raggedy ship
Here we go, on this death trip

Packed in ships
Worse than sardines
Filled in a can
Children, elders
Woman and man

From our beautiful home
The place of our birth
To distant shores
Hell holes of the Earth

Many unfed
And brutally treated
Chained like animals
With beatings repeated

A journey of 2 months
On average they say
Nothing but tortures
Each day after day

Kings, Queens and Warriors
Once standing so brave
Shrunk down to nothing

Soon to be slaves

Crick Crack that raggedy ship
Here we go on this death trip

Left in own urine
Vomit and feces
Families broken
Left there in pieces

Pinned to ships floorboards
Tearing skin to the bone
All could be heard
Were the screams and the moans

Buck breaking they say
Begun on the ships
Evident to see…
Their perversions
So sick!

Why would a person?
Want to rape any man?
With regards to this matter
Rape any hue-man?

Praying for rough seas
Which would give some a break
From inhumane abuses
No person should take

Crick Crack that raggedy ship
Here we go on this death trip

Blinded by the sunlight
When brought up for water
But for many it was time
For the lamb to the slaughter

Some took chances overboard
Rather'd to be eaten by sharks
So don't say we allowed it
Please save those remarks

All could be done
Was to plan an escape
And at the right time
To make a quick break

Some luckily escaped
But many did not
Some swam and ran
Some sadly got shot

But some got free
With beneficial avail
They live on in us
To tell the tales

Crick Crack that raggedy ship
How we survived
That **gruesome** death trip!

5: LOOK TO AFRICA/ALKEBULAN

Lands so lust and green
Others with waterfalls
Of the greatest Serene
Knowledge of Babylon

To Timbuktu
Orders so great that only some knew

Ancient's civilizations of immense spirituality
For all who are wise, this is the reality
Remember the greatest
Inventions of worth
Call to Mama Africa
Alkebulan! The place of all births

6: ANCESTORS

To All Ancestors of Love and light
To All Ancestors who tried to do right…
To All Ancestors who fought for liberation
To All Ancestors who suffered great tribulation

To All Ancestors who were murdered, raped and pillaged
To All Ancestors who constantly dreamt of their village
To All Ancestors so slender and lean
To All Ancestors the Great Kings and Great Queens

To All Ancestors who strived to be free
To All of the Ancestors
Who did it for me!

WE REMEMBER YOU!

7: HERE HE COMES!

No! No! Not Again!

Here he comes
That filthy scum
Leaving his wife
To get him some

MASSA: Where's the wench?
MOTHER: Who you talkin' 'bout sir?

MASSA: Who you think? Marabelle...
                Now go get the whore!

MASSA: Tell her to meet me
                In the barn
                She better be quick...
                So there's no harm!

                He left the cabin
                With a cheeky grin
                She's only 13...
                Now- What a sin

CHILD: Don't worry Mama
                It will be quick
MOTHER: My darling baby ...

I feel so sick

So she leaves the cabin
So bold and so brave
It was a daily practice
To rape a slave

Rape of a man
Woman or child
Is something one
Could never describe

It was for sure
A daily practice
Only satan himself
Would ever back this

The barn door creeks
The innocent is dragged
And flung to the ground
By the satanic old hag

So the raping begins
Of this innocent soul
By this disgusting beast
Who has no form of control

If she had a knife
She would kill them all
Yet this devil brute

Was having a ball

He's finally finished
And gets up to leave
And all she could do
Was to Heave! And Heave!

Vomit after Vomit
From the stench and the act
He needs to be dead
As a matter of fact

She ran back to her cabin
Crying with shame
Mama holds her and says:

MOTHER: You're not to blame

This is part of your life
As that of a slave
And somehow
My baby …
You'll find a way
To be brave

Mama sets the bath
With plenty of herbs
With boiling hot water
To settle the nerves

She sings her a lullaby

Which travelled from Africa
She remembers it so well
Before her capture in Ghana

She washes away the hurt and the pain

Singing:

(EWE)	(ENGLISH)
Tutu gbɔvi	Don't cry little child
Tutu gbɔvi	Don't cry little child
Nana me le aƒea	Your mother isn't home
Meke ola fa vi na	Who are you crying for?
Ao dzedze vinye	My poor little child
Bɔnu bɔnu kpoo	Please sleep peacefully

The hurt and pain
Is washed away
Nonetheless…
It is left…
To see…
Another day!

8: JUMPING THE BROOM

It's the day to jump the broom
And everyone is there
Daisy-Mae and Toby-Brown
Such a beautiful pair

Quietly and in Secret
Friends and family gather round
Beyond two plantations
African love was truly found

The women dress the bride
And the men counsel the groom
Hidden from the Massa
They are sure to be married soon

We're all gathered here today
To not just stand and watch
But to continuously hope and pray
While this couple ties the knot

To bless and to guide this couple
On this sacred day
And whenever in doubt or trouble
To the ancestors they must pray

The reason why we're marrying

Daisy-Mae and Toby-Crow
Better known as:
Queen Akina and Warrior King Cudjoe

A couple that had against all odds
Have found each other from Ghana
Despite being sold away from each other
They have managed to stay together

They say that freedom is close at hand
A time we all wait to honour
Continuing our unions as we design
Let no man can put asunder

She is a Queen and you a King
This is whom we are marrying

Treasure each other
Always and forever
And once again
Please do remember…

That freedom will be coming soon
 Now go ahead …
And "Jump the Broom!"

9: SUN UP TO SUNDOWN

Just imagine...
Sunup to Sundown, in the fields picking cotton
Sunup to Sundown, constantly whipped by the Massa
Sunup to Sundown, weighed down by Shackles
Then the auction block for me

Sunup to Sundown, children being sold
Sunup to Sundown, continuously controlled
Sunup to Sundown, sometimes left to die
Sunup to Sundown, the Mistress telling lies

Sunup to Sundown, trying to be brave
Sunup to Sundown, only you the slave
Sunup to Sundown, spirits running high
Sunup to Sundown, Massa has to die

Sunup to Sundown, Mama being raped
Sunup to Sundown, Papa's head on a stake
Sunup to Sundown, lessons to be learned
Sunup to Sundown, plantations have to burn

Sunup to Sundown, looking back when we were free
Sunup to Sundown, wanting Africa to be me
Sunup to Sundown, Africa in my bones
Sunup to Sun down, looking to Africa my home!

10: THE REAL MOSES

"Make one sound, and you all get killed."
"I'm the Massa of this gun, undoubtedly skilled!"
"I'm not prepared to lose not one of you!"
By then we knew we had to pursue.

Through the hot sun and treacherous snow,
You just can't imagine, it was quite a show.
Babies held underwater when horses were heard,
No one made a sound, not one single word.

It was hard to believe how babies did not drown,
She held them underwater for fear of the sound.
She walked them on, for more than a month,
From the South to the North, it had to be done.

Back and forth she continuously went,
Making many trips not leaving a scent.
Risking it all, with not even a ship,
Fearing nothing nor no one,
Not even the whip.

Hundreds were freed,
By this great liberator.
They tried so hard,
To eliminate her.

The ancestral Moses,
Who was never afraid.
Mama Harriet Tubman,
Our Moses…
Please remember her name!

11: PICKING COTTON

The cock crows and up we go
To the cotton fields
To pick the load!

The back-breaking task
And hands full of sores,
We had to make sure
That we made the scores.

We picked 200 pounds
At minimum a day,
And as you well know
There was never no pay.

Not for the enslaved
Now that's for sure,
All for Massa
To even the score.

Of what he owed
To other Plantations,
Leaving no debt
For his generations.

Then there was us
The enslaved Africans,

Left to fight over
Half-eaten rations.

But time will tell
What is in store,
For the cotton pickers
Who picked cotton galore.

The scars of the whip
Tearing through layers of flesh,
Oh the strain and the pain
Of psychological and physical stress.

How can anyone
Treat another so cold?
Only the devil by nature
Would let another be sold.

Without any remorse
Just left there to die,
Like a raisin in the sun
Left out there to dry.

Oh how we remember
The cotton fields,
And the young one's
Putting out an appeal.

When the elders
Hadn't met the day's quota,

Pleading to Massa
With enhanced diploma.

Begging and pleading
To give the elders a break,
Massa would shout:
"Continue!!!
Or get tied to the stake!"

What evil demons
One cannot deny,
Picking cotton wasn't easy
Someday... You try!

12: THE BIG HOUSE

How we hated to work
In the plantation house
Removed from being hue-man
To less than a mouse

Massa and his wife
Watching your every move
Fetch this! Fetch that!
A punch a kick
Just constant abuse

The stench of Massa's wife…
She's seriously scared of water
The rape of boys and girls
African sons and daughters

The amount of enslaved fainting
Just from the stench
Yet they have the cheek
To call us Queens the wench

Then Massa would come
With his pale stinking self
Not even a bath
Despite all of his wealth

Imagine…

Having that nasty scum
Take you when he wanted
Next thing you're breeding
Which left you real haunted

The herbs of our elders
Kept pregnancy at bay
They would do their magic potions
Which made one bleed for days

And when it was done
Being finally over
It was now time for us
To become the controller

Other herbs would be used
In Massa and Mistress food
A slow poisoning for sure
Which sure changed their mood

Slowly but surly
They would become sicker and sicker
A slow and painful death
For those two wicked Niggers!!!

13: RESISTANCE AND REBELLION

Resistance and Rebellion was in our nature
From free in Mama Africa right to the capture
We would kick, punch, scratch and bite
Resisting as we could, with all of our might

We would strangle the catchers
With their own chains
But guns were mightier than the spears
So at times resisting in vain

We resisted and rebelled
Week after week
Rebellion and resistance
Was no place for the meek

On the ships
We jumped overboard
Desiring suicide at large
On some successful attempts
We would take charge

Like the Amistad,
Just one ship to mention
Overthrowing the captain and crew
Which soon got the attention

On plantations we did runaways
A daily activity
For the captured African
Who would die for their liberty

Suicides and poisoning
Was a usual thing
Who the hell was Bukkra?
To tie up any King

We used the drum
To communicate with others
On plantations near and far…
They were our sisters and brothers

During all trying times
We would burn down plantations
Remember 1791 …
The revolt by the Haitians?

What about Nat Turner
The greatest of all
He knew all too well
That they all had to fall

He said:

"Spare no one,
Not man, woman, nor child
As we know that these demons

Will oppress us with pride

Kill them all …
Let none get away
For today we remember
Our ancestor's names!"

And there you have the house Negroes
Who would poison them all
By putting poisonous herbs in food
No matter how small

So we continuously resisted
With what fate would allow
And we never stopped resisting
From then until now!

14: THE MAROONS

The Maroons! The Maroons!
The greatest of all
From the Americas
To the Caribbean
They refused to fall

They would run into mountains
Claiming their territories
Building resistance armies
Of warriors, some Ashanti(s)

Nanny was the most famous of all
It was said she was tiny, extremely small
She was known as a grand magician
Always maintaining her stance
Without any submission
She would kill with a glance

Enslaved from Ghana to Jamaica
She was known to catch bullets
Alongside her brother Cudjoe
Europeans knew not to push it

She could go invisible
In the middle of the day
Then appear in the hills

Near her hideaways

From 1728 to 1739
They declared war
Against the British
Who were well out of line

The Maroons could not be defeated
The Europeans wanted Nanny dead
This was never going to happen
So they signed a peace treaty instead

This allowed the governments
To leave the maroons alone
And as a result, up to this day
Maroon Town is their home!

15: AUCTION BLOCK

Poking and pricking
Sticking and kicking
Mouth pulled open
But nothing is spoken

Tongue poked out
Teethe are clenched
Hips are inspected
To make a good wench

Breasts are felt roughly
Words whispered softly
"I'm buying you…
You will make me so happy!"

The greatest of warriors
Looking so weak and so frail
The disgrace in their hearts
Only they know the tales

Women giggling and lusting
Over these men
Such a pitiful sight
One looked around ten

I heard one say:

"I'm in for a treat…
What a beautiful specimen
A fine piece of meat."

The abuse all would face
When they hit the plantations
Someone please rescue those

From The Great African Nations!

16: THE FOOT WARMER

On the cold chilly night
Not a soul insight
Who would warm?
Massa's feet tonight

Oh yes…the foot warmer

MASSA:

Matilda-Sue!
Go and call your brother
Be sure it's him
And not no other

MATILDA-SUE:

Yes Massa Sir
I shall go right away
Your feet must be
Mighty cold today

MATILDA-SUE:

Little Joe! Little Joe!
Get out of bed
No more sleep for you
Go warm Massa's feet instead

Little Joe jumps up
Out of his sleep
It's time to give
Massa's feet some heat

He arrives at the big house
So frail and so scared
To all of us
That seems extremely weird

Joe curls on the floor
Like a little mouse
On the ice-cold floor
Of the Plantation house

Massa puts his cold feet
On little Joes back
Drawing the heat out of him
Just to be exact

Then says....

MASSA: You're the best foot warmer
                    I ever done had,
                    For buying you boy,
                    I am mighty glad

                    When I am warm little Joe
                    You can go back to bed:
MASSA: Did you hear me Little-Joe?

LITTLE-JOE: Yes Massa, he said

17: THE BABY NEEDS A' FEEDIN

MISTRESS JONES: Hattie! Hattie!
                  Can't you hear the baby screaming?

                  What took you so long?
                  The baby needs a feedin'

HATTIE-MAE: I'm sorry Mistress Jones
                  I was feeding my son
MISTRESS JONES: You leave him to someone else
                  Before mine is left with none

                  Now listen to me Hattie girl-
                  You full well know the rules!
                  Mistress baby always gets fed first
                  So don't you play no fool!

HATTIE-MAE: I'm so sorry Mistress Jones
                  But my baby was so hungry
MISTRESS JONES: No one cares about your baby girl
                  You know who runs this country!

                  So don't you dare, ever get smart
                  Or you'll be off for a whipping
                   When you finish feeding Lilly-white
                  Hurry back to that kitchen!

HATTIE-MAE: But Mistress Maam…
                 I'm begging you
                 Can I please feed my son?
MISTRESS JONES: Did you not hear me
                 Wet Nurse Hattie-Mae!
                 There's work to be done!

18- WHAT A BUCK

Oh my what a Buck

Those strapping shoulders
Built like boulders
And not to mention
That big strong back

"What's your name?" she asks
"Strong Burrow" he answers
"Well listen here boy…
 Come and see me tomorrow."

"Tomorrow I can't Maam…
So much work to do
What if we get caught?
And Massa knew?"

"Oh listen Burrow
Don't you pay him no mind
Massa won't be back
'til well after nine"

"Make sure you're on time
And don't you worry,
If you turn up late
You will be sorry."

"How I can't wait
To hold you so,
Your chocolate skin
Like dark Cocoa."

"So just hurry Burrow
Cause we can't get caught,
For if we are
I'll do what's taught."

"If you're Massa comes early
You know the fate,
I'll have no choice
But to holla out rape!"

19- CHRONICLES OF THE ENSLAVED

Stolen and taken
To far away shores,
With the title of slaves
Niggers and whores.
Ripped of all dignity
In these faraway lands,
Classified less than an animal
Not a hue-man.
Hung...Lynched
And whipped to the bone,
You're no longer kin
Not even your own.
All rights you have lost
To the owners of you,
Now a commodity
Owned by a few.
How could this be?
If man is of man,
So easy if you're classed
As less than hue-man!

20: MASSA PLEASE...NOT MY BABY

BANG! BANG!

MARYBELLE: Morning Massa Fields
How you seem to be doing?

MASSA FIELDS: You ain't goin' like this Marybelle
Baby-Belle is up for a viewing

MARYBELLE: No Massa Please!
She's the only one I got!

MASSA FIELDS: I know Marybelle
But she sure is worth a lot

MARYBELLE: But Please! Massa, Please!
She's only two years old!
Please Massa Fields!
All the others you done sold!

MASSA FIELDS: Oh dear Marybelle...
It must be really hard
But we breed you all for profit
Anything else we disregard

So go and get her ready
I'll be back for her in a minute
Be sure to say a full goodbye
She'll remain with you in spirit

MARYBELLE: But Please! Massa Please!
                  At least leave me with one?
MASSA FIELDS: Marybelle
                  You've been here
                  Time before
                  Just get her ready…
                  Now!! It's done!!!

21: THE DRUM

Can you hear it?
Can you feel it?
Can you hear it?
The beat! The beat!

It's hard to hear them
And not be swayed
To the rhythm of the drum
And how it's played

The message it sends
To young and old
How it feeds the spirit
One's very soul

Can you hear it?
Can you feel it?
Can you hear it?
The beat! The beat!

The Yoruba drums
And djembes too
Are sure to play
A tune for you

Used for upliftment

Empowerment and Strength
As well as for messages
From plantations sent

Can you hear it?
Can you feel it?
Can you hear it?
The beat! The beat!

Vibrations that echo
Loud and clear
In the moonlit nights
With stars so near

Lost in the rhythms
That never grow old
The tones arranged
That feed the soul

Can you hear it?
Can you feel it?
Can you hear it?
The beat, The beat!

Can you hear it?
Can you feel it?
Can you hear it?
That Beat, So Sweet!

22: LIBATION

The drums sounds while we all gather
Deep in the woods, huddled together

In secrecy this gathering unfolds
To embrace the ancestors
The young to the old

Those gone before us
Now on spiritual planes
Guiding, protecting
We honour their names

The priests and the priestesses
Gather some water
We call on the names
 Of each son and each daughter

This all takes place
Within the midnight hours
We ask for protection
From the Almighty's powers

We remember the Earth
So that seedlings will grow
The rivers and seas
And the wind breeze that blows

Remembering all things
In this great Universe
Mama Africa- we decree
One must always immerse

23: STRANGE FRUIT

There's a strange fruit in the Poplar tree
Who could it be? Who could it be?
Such a strange fruit in the Poplar tree

The runaway,
Sadly got caught
Dragged back to the plantation
So cruelly brought

All slaves are called
To gather 'round
Everyone must look
At whom had been found

There's a strange fruit in the Poplar tree
Who could it be? Who could it be?
Such a strange fruit in the Poplar tree

The noose is tied
Around the neck
The other end tied
To the horse's sack
Suddenly…
The whip is cracked
Right across
The horses back

There's a strange fruit in the Poplar tree
Who could it be? Who could it be?
Such a strange fruit in the Poplar tree

Then left their dangling
Jerking once or twice
Massa smirking
As cold as ice

The enslaved
Witnessing another hanging
For which it was
Never-ending

That brave soul Kunta
Left to hang there
For all to watch
To continue the fear
Of what would happen
If another should run
Even animals are free
Much less a hue-man

Kunta's Mother watching
With immense pain
Also his wife
Poor Mary-Jane
To Massa he was
Just a Nigger

All this meant now
He would breed
Wenches quicker

There's a strange fruit in the Poplar tree
Who could it be? Who could it be?
Such a strange fruit in the Poplar tree

24: 15 LASHES

SLAVE:

Please! Please! Miss Laura-Mae
I beg you please! Don't make me pay
You slapped me so extremely harsh
And made me slip and break that glass

MISTRESS:

You should've been more careful
You Negroe B**ch
Go by the tree
I'll get the whip

Be at the whipping tree
I shall meet you there
You negro wench
As if I care

You'll get 15 strikes
With my whip
Let's see if Massa
Still wants those hips

He looks at you
And never at me
A Negro wench
How could this be?

Just looking and lusting
All over you

And you're as black as tar
With that big butt too

When he sees you
He has no control
And your hair so nappy
Can't be flicked in a bow

For this for sure
I will make you pay
You'll have 15 lashes
Everyday!

25: FREEDOM

What does freedom smell or taste like?
Can someone please tell me?

You see….
My Ma and Pa came from a place called Africa!
Where they say that they were free
They were singing, laughing, playing and dancing
Oh what thoughts, I just can't imagine

And here we are
Told when to wake...
Owned by beings
So full of hate

Told when to sleep
And when to eat
When to laugh
And when to weep

Ma speaks about fufu
Sweet plantains and fish
The pounding of yams
Oh my! What a dish!

Here we are given
Little bits to eat

Like cow foot and tripe
Rotting leftover meats

Pittance of foods
To barely keep us alive
With no nutritional value
Yet we survive

Pa says: "By having to make do…"

A little of this
And a little of that
Hiding knowledge of self
Now ain't that a fact

Then Africa beaten out of you
Ensuring you could never pursue
A faraway place
For one and all to roam
That place they call Africa
My Ma and Pa's home!

26: HOW TO MAKE A SLAVE

MASSA:

You better than her
She's so black
Leave the cotton-picking
Let Black Betty do that

And look at her hair
It's so nappy and thick
It's not silky like yours
So you make her sick

MASSA:

Toby boy,
You're getting too old
Call young Tom
To carry the load

TOBY:

But Massa Willie
I won't have anything to do
You know I've always
Been good to you

MASSA:

Lou-Lou Mae
You're looking grand
Something Big-George
Won't understand

LOU-LOU MAE:

Pardon for asking

MASSA:

What do you mean Massa?
Just look at his idiocy
He's a sure disaster

Don't worry too much
Y'all can depend on me
I feed you and clothe you
I do it for free

REBELLIOUS JOE:

Now!!!
Hear me good
And hear me well
That evil Massa Will
Got us all living in hell

Not one of y'all listen
To that wicked old Grinch
He's trying to divide us:
Evil Massa, Willie Lynch!

27: MULATTO

Who can trust a Mulatto?

The Mulatto girl
The Mulatto boy
Being the product
From Massa's joy

Birthed from a wench
Who mistress would hate
The final end product
From constant rape

She feels that she's better
No matter the weather
And that being high yellow
Highers her stake

She looks down on others
With full African blood
She would rather be Mulatto
Than a true royal one

She does not understand
Why she's working the fields
With the Negro slaves
Who have no free will

When Massa is home
She can work in the house
A little entitlement
He may sometimes allow

Still not understanding
When Massa's away
It is back to the fields
To work cotton or cane

She thinks that she's privileged
When in Massa's big house
Not minding the abuse
From the disgust of his spouse

Cooking and cleaning
And washing her clothes
Being a slave
To someone you loathed

Mistress spitting
And kicking her
Day after day
She could not careless
She's the Mulatto slave

Oh Mulatto! Mulatto!
I wish you'd imagine
How your Ma loves you more

Though not born out of passion

So my sweet Mulatto dear
Come close please and listen

Please take some time
To go 'head and figure

To everything white
Whether father or mother
Mulatto Child
You're just another Nigger!

28: THE STENCH! THE STENCH!

Oh My Lawd!
The Stench! The Stench!
That makes me clench
My very breath

Oh My Lawd!
The Stench! The Stench!
Massa and his wife
Smells like rotting flesh

The stench in the winter
So imagine when sun
You just can't wait
'Til your work is done

Oh My Gosh!
The Stench! The Stench!
That makes me clench
My very breath!

29: LABOUR PAINS

It's all happening now
Mistress giving birth
No one really cares
For all that it's worth

Massa is so happy
The first heir to his nation
I bet he won't be selling his kin
To Massa Smiths plantation

Push! Mistress Push!
I can nearly see the head!
Just do it Mistress Push!
Just go on right ahead!

Massa lighting his cigar
As it's finally going to happen
Smiling like a cheshire cat
How his heart is filled with passion

So Push! Mistress Push!
The head is to be birthed
Hold up!
Wait a Minute…
What… On… Earth…

Massa came rushing in
When he heard the baby cry
He stood so still in shock and horror:
Then Screamed:
"This Nigga baby ain't mine!"

Tribute to my Ancestors by:
Nyah-Chanti Parker (9 years old)

30: BECAUSE OF MY ANCESTORS!

Because of my Ancestors
I wake in the morning

Because of my Ancestors
I can run without warning

Because of my Ancestors
I can live my life

Because of my Ancestors
I can see the light

Because of my Ancestors
I have a place to be

Because of my Ancestors
I am not hung from a tree

Because of my Ancestors
I am free to be me

Nyah-Chanti Parker

31: THINK

Do you ever wonder what it would be?
If we were left on the continent
In pastures so green?
As free as the birds, just left to sore
Above the highest terrains for all to adore

Going through rites of passages
The transitions of life
Then meeting your ordained
Husband or even your wife
Do you ever wonder?
What it would be
If we were left on the continent
In pastures so green?

Plantain, Mangoes, Coconuts galore
No such thing as Mcdonalds or KFC
That's for sure
Natural herbs and spices
Dried in the Sun
No family going hungry,
Not ever- not one
Do you ever wonder?
What it would be
If we were left on the continent
In pastures so green?

Children playing happily
Laughing all-day
Listening to the stories
That came into play
Of how we once were
And the importance of cultures
To protect the traditions
From those- culture stealing vultures
Do you ever wonder?
What it would be
If we were left on the continent
In pastures so green?

Do you ever wonder?
How the West was won?
And how the destruction
Of African civilizations begun?

Kemet, Songhai and Timbuktu
We could go on
But that's just a few

Take a minute to think ....
What would it be?
If YOU were left on the continent
In pastures so green?

32: I AM NOT A SLAVE

I am not a slave
But one who was enslaved
I am not a slave
But one who was so brave

I am not a slave
But the God and Goddess
Of the Earth

I am not a slave
But the Cream of the Universe!

Remember: "Cream always rises to the top"

33: REMEMBER

Always remember–
You are not a slave
But the essence of those warriors
So bold
And so brave

Against all odds
You survived it all
So stand high, stand high!
Forever stand tall!

You came from great Kingdoms
Of Sophistication
Knowledge and Wealth
The Leaders of Maths and Medicine
So people please know thyself

In the next series of poems
We shall relate
Speaking of our great Kingdoms
To put the record straight

Now remember who you are
You Great Queens and Great kings
Take your rightful places
And let your reign begin !

Aṣe! Aṣe! Aṣe!

COMING SOON

STRAIGHT

Book Two of the Poetic trilogy by THE ANCESTORS continuing to relate to the experiences of people of African Heritage will be called: STRAIGHT. Book two fo the triology will be exploring the Pre-African holocaust era. Where African people ruled, the Great Kingdoms of Kemet, Mali, Ghana and Songhai and their great contributions to the world.

Printed in Great Britain
by Amazon